SUPER
SANDCASTLE·
Animal Habitats

What Lives in Antarctica?

Oona Gaarder-Juntti

Consulting Editor, Diane Craig, M.A./Reading Specialist

ABDO
Publishing Company

3 1800 00258 3108

Published by ABDO Publishing Company, 8000 West 78th Street, Edina, Minnesota 55439. Copyright © 2009 by Abdo Consulting Group, Inc. International copyrights reserved in all countries. No part of this book may be reproduced in any form without written permission from the publisher. Super SandCastle™ is a trademark and logo of ABDO Publishing Company.

Printed in the United States.

Credits
Editor: Liz Salzmann
Content Developer: Nancy Tuminelly
Cover and Interior Design and Production: Oona Gaarder-Juntti, Mighty Media
Illustration: Oona Gaarder-Juntti
Photo Credits: AbleStock, Creatas, Eyewire, Jamie Hall, I Everson/WWI/S.Muller/ PeterArnold Inc., ShutterStock

Library of Congress Cataloging-in-Publication Data

Gaarder-Juntti, Oona, 1979-

What lives in Antarctica? / Oona Gaarder-Juntti.

p. cm. -- (Animal habitats)

ISBN 978-1-60453-169-5

1. Zoology--Antarctica--Juvenile literature. 2. Animals--Antarctica--Juvenile literature. I. Title.

QL106.G33 2008

591.70911'6--dc22

2008011395

Super SandCastle™ books are created by a team of professional educators, reading specialists, and content developers around five essential components— phonemic awareness, phonics, vocabulary, text comprehension, and fluency— to assist young readers as they develop reading skills and strategies and increase their general knowledge. All books are written, reviewed, and leveled for guided reading, early reading intervention, and Accelerated Reader® programs for use in shared, guided, and independent reading and writing activities to support a balanced approach to literacy instruction.

About SUPER SANDCASTLE™

Bigger Books for Emerging Readers
Grades K–4

Created for library, classroom, and at-home use, Super SandCastle™ books support and engage young readers as they develop and build literacy skills and will increase their general knowledge about the world around them. Super SandCastle™ books are part of SandCastle™, the leading PreK–3 imprint for emerging and beginning readers. Super SandCastle™ features a larger trim size for more reading fun.

Let Us Know
Super SandCastle™ would like to hear your stories about reading this book. What was your favorite page? Was there something hard that you needed help with? Share the ups and downs of learning to read. We want to hear from you! Send us an e-mail.

sandcastle@abdopublishing.com

Contact us for a complete list of SandCastle™, Super SandCastle™, and other nonfiction and fiction titles from ABDO Publishing Company.

www.abdopublishing.com • 8000 West 78th Street Edina, MN 55439 • 800-800-1312 • 952-831-1632 fax

Antarctica is the fifth largest continent. It is the coldest, driest, and windiest place on earth. 97 percent of Antarctica is covered by snow and ice.

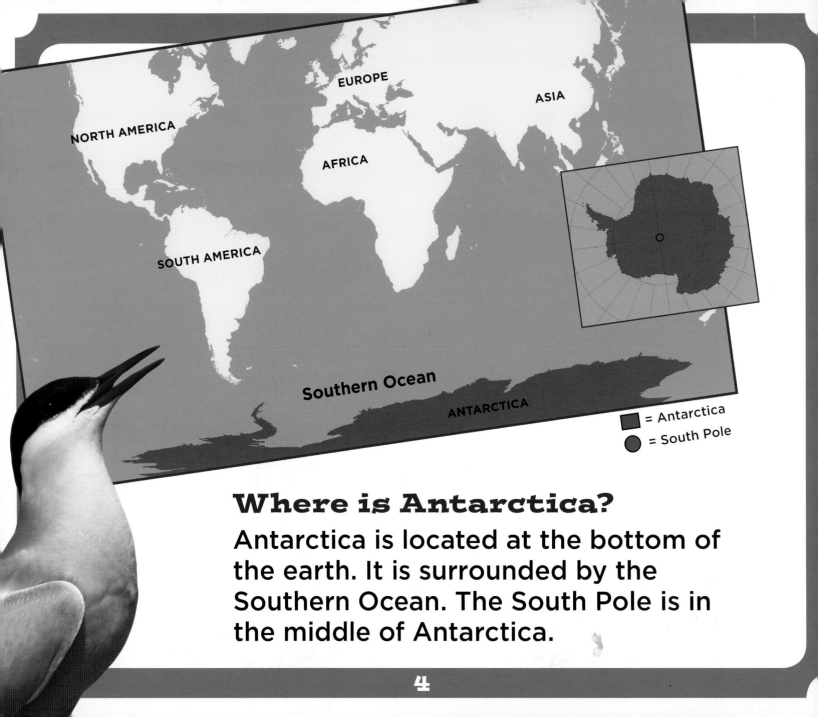

= Antarctica

= South Pole

Where is Antarctica?

Antarctica is located at the bottom of the earth. It is surrounded by the Southern Ocean. The South Pole is in the middle of Antarctica.

What does Antarctica look like?

Antarctica is covered by a thick layer of ice. 90 percent of all the ice on earth is located here. Most Antarctic animals live near the coast or in the Southern Ocean.

ANTARCTIC KRILL

Animal class: Invertebrate
Location: Southern Ocean

Antarctic krill are small shrimp-like creatures that live in the sea. They are an important food for other animals. Fish, squid, penguins, seals, and whales all eat krill.

Billions of Antarctic krill gather in huge swarms that cover hundreds of miles.

7

BLUE-EYED SHAG

Animal class: Bird
Location: Antarctica and Southern Ocean

Blue-eyed shags have bright blue skin around their eyes. They eat fish and krill. Blue-eyed shags are good divers. They swim underwater to catch fish.

Blue-eyed shags build their nests on land. Unlike other Antarctic birds, they don't like being on the ice.

CHINSTRAP PENGUIN

Animal class: Bird
Location: Antarctica and Southern Ocean

The chinstrap penguin is named for the thin black line that runs under its chin. Chinstrap penguins live and breed in large colonies. They make their nests out of rocks.

Chinstrap penguins shed their feathers every year and grow new ones. They don't eat or swim during this time.

10

EMPEROR PENGUIN

Animal class: Bird
Location: Antarctica and Southern Ocean

Emperor penguins are the largest penguins. They are about 45 inches tall and weigh up to 90 pounds. Male penguins keep the eggs warm. The females get food for the chicks.

Emperor penguin colonies are located on the ice. They stand close together to stay warm.

Antarctic Fur Seal

Animal class: Mammal
Location: Antarctica and Southern Ocean

Fur seals have an outer coat of rough fur. They have an undercoat of soft fur that is waterproof. Fur seals eat krill, fish, and squid. They dive at night to feed.

Fur seals have four large flippers. They use their flippers to walk around on land.

Central Islip Public Library
33 Hawthorne Avenue
Central Islip, NY 11722

15

SOUTHERN ELEPHANT SEAL

Animal class: Mammal
Location: Antarctica and Southern Ocean

Southern elephant seals are the largest seals. Males can be 20 feet long and weigh 8,000 pounds or more! They can dive over 5,000 feet deep and stay under for up to two hours.

Males have a large, curved nose like an elephant's trunk. Their nose helps them roar loudly.

ORCA

Animal class: Mammal
Location: All oceans

Orcas are the largest member of the dolphin family. Orcas can swim up to 30 miles per hour to catch their prey. Orcas hunt fish, sea turtles, sharks, squid, penguins, and seals.

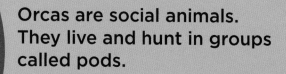

Orcas are social animals. They live and hunt in groups called pods.

HUMPBACK WHALE

Animal class: Mammal
Location: All oceans

Humpback whales often leap out of the water and land on their backs. This is called breaching. Humpbacks can make many different sounds. They sometimes sing for hours at a time.

A humpback's tail fin can be up to 18 feet wide. Every humpback has different markings on its tail.

Have you ever been to Antarctica?

More Antarctic Animals

Can you learn about these Antarctic animals?

Adélie penguin

Antarctic petrel

Antarctic skua

arctic tern

blue whale

crabeater seal

gentoo penguin

giant squid

king penguin

leopard seal

macaroni penguin

minke whale

rockhopper penguin

sperm whale

Weddell seal

Glossary

billion – a very large number. One billion is also written 1,000,000,000.

breed – to create offspring, or babies.

colony – a group of animals or plants that live or grow together.

continent – one of seven large land masses on earth. The continents are Asia, Africa, Europe, North America, South America, Australia, and Antarctica.

female – being of the sex that can produce eggs or give birth. Mothers are female.

flipper – a wide, flat limb of a sea creature, such as a seal or a dolphin, that is used for swimming.

invertebrate – a creature that does not have a spine.

male – being of the sex that can father offspring. Fathers are male.

mammal – a warm-blooded animal that has hair and whose females produce milk to feed the young.

marking – the pattern of color on an animal.

shed – to lose something, such as skin, leaves, or fur, through a natural process.

shrimp – a small shellfish often caught for food.

trunk – an elephant's upper lip and long nose.

MAR 18 2009

CENTRAL ISLIP PUBLIC LIBRARY

3 1800 00258 3108

258 3108

J591.
709
GAA

Gaarder-Juntti, Oona

What Lives in Antarctica?

$15.95

Central Islip Public Library
33 Hawthorne Avenue
Central Islip, NY 11722-2498

GAYLORD M